TRENDS

RENNAY CRAATS

Weigl Publishers Inc.

Published by Weigl Publishers Inc.
350 5th Avenue, Suite 3304, PMB 6G
New York, NY 10118-0069
Website: www.weigl.com

Library of Congress Cataloging-in-Publication Data

Craats, Rennay.
 Trends : USA past, present, future / Rennay Craats.
    p. cm.
 Includes index.
 ISBN 978-1-59036-976-0 (hard cover : alk. paper) -- ISBN 978-1-59036-977-7 (soft cover : alk. paper)
 1. United States--Civilization--Juvenile literature. 2. Social change--United States--Juvenile literature. I.
Title.
 E169.1.C798 2009
 973--dc22
                                    2008023864

Printed in the United States of America
1 2 3 4 5 6 7 8 9 0 12 11 10 09 08

EDITOR: Heather C. Hudak
DESIGN: Terry Paulhus

Trends
Contents

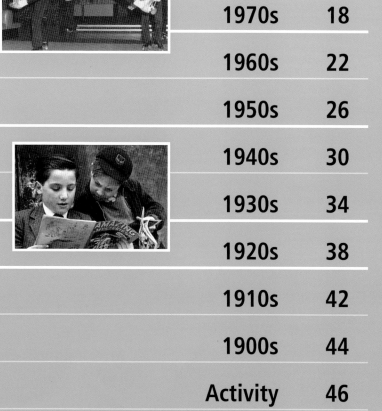

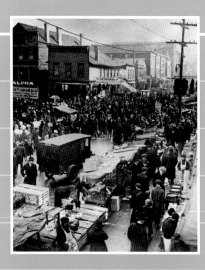

Trends
Through The Years

Since the beginning of the 20th century, the American economy has faced massive challenges and achieved great successes. As part of this ever-changing economy, certain items have become wildly popular, spurring people across the nation to take action.

The word "trend" is defined as something that is developing or changing in an upward or downward direction. It often refers to products, people, or events that experience incredible success for a period of time. In many cases, trends are unique items that impress people with their creativity. They may be as simple as the hula hoop or as complex as the hippie movement. Regardless, trends may fade as quickly as they appear.

Throughout U.S. history, thousands of toys, hairstyles, fashions, events, songs, dances, and television shows have touched every part of our lives. From the Jennifer Aniston haircut of the 1990s to Cabbage Patch Kids and Crocs, there has been something to appeal to all tastes across this vast nation. Everyone has witnessed or taken part in helping at least one item become a trend.

Trends are uncertain. It is often difficult to determine how or why something gains such mass popularity. However, it is certain that new trends will continue to rise and fall for all of time.

2000

Personal Area Networks

As technology becomes more powerful and more efficient, devices can become smaller and more portable. Many devices now are lightweight and easily carried, such as cellular phones, personal music players, digital organizers, and **global positioning systems** (GPS).

Often, these devices are connected to one another through specialized signals. In the 1990s, a company called Ericsson developed a type of signal known as Bluetooth. The signal is fast and uses very little power, helping to extend the life of the batteries used in many portable devices. By 2000, products were being developed to use with this technology.

Using a Bluetooth connection, a laptop computer can connect to the Internet through a cell phone. In the same way, a digital mapping device can email directions or information about a specific location through its connection to an organizer. These wireless connections between small, portable devices are sometimes referred to as a Personal Area Network, or PAN. High-speed, low-power connections, such as Bluetooth, help people organize information easily.

Personal Area Networks

2001

Jimmy Wales starts the website Wikipedia.

2002

Camera phones become available to the North American public.

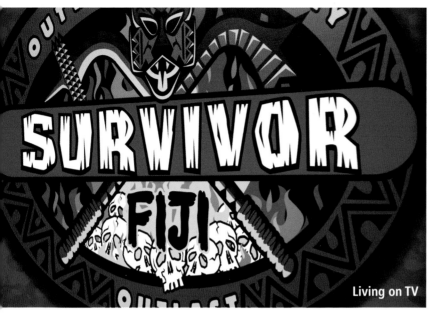

Living on TV

2001

Game On

Video games were first introduced to the public in the early 1970s. Since then, they have continued to grow in popularity. In 2001, the video game industry in the United States claimed $9.4 billion in sales. Improvements in technology allowed video games to contain more detailed artwork, complex plots and stories, CD-quality music, and spoken dialogue. One year after it was launched in 2006, Nintendo's Wii was the most purchased video game system in the world. Online games also became popular, as game designers took advantage of the Internet to connect players from around the world.

2000

Living on TV

In 2000, reality TV hit the airwaves in a big way. One of the most watched shows on television, *Survivor*, featured real people in largely unscripted situations. Adding to the popularity of this show was the fact the the contestants were competing in extreme conditions and vying for an incredibly large sum of money. On *Survivor*, contestants are sent to an **uninhabited** tropical island, where they compete against one another to stay on the island the longest. The last person on the island wins all of the prize money. Today, reality TV has become part of everyday programming. From *The Bachelor* to *Deal, or No Deal*, shows that star people who have agreed to be filmed in unusual situations are commonplace. Many popular reality shows follow ordinary people as they remodel their houses, try to become fit, build motorcycles, tackle odd jobs, and carry out science experiments.

Game On

2003
Movie star Arnold Schwarzenegger becomes governor of California.

2004
Livestrong bracelets become popular.

2005
TiVo gains popularity as a digital video recorder.

7

Heroic Cinema

Victoria Beckham

2002

Heroic Cinema

In the 1950s, 1960s and 1970s, comic book superheroes, such as Superman, Batman, the X-Men, and Spider-Man, became household names. In the 2000s, Hollywood turned these popular heroes into movie stars. The movie *Spider-Man*, released in 2002, was one of the most popular superhero movies of all time. Many other superhero movies followed this technique of updating and re-explaining the origins of superheroes for modern audiences. In 2005, new Batman and Superman movies were released, as well as *V for Vendetta*. All three movies were well-received by audiences and critics. It seemed that, in the 2000s, it was time for comic books to move from the page to the screen.

2006

Victoria Beckham trades her long hair for a short crop, creating a fashion trend.

2007

The iPhone hits the market.

2008

Shoes with square toes and thick, chunky heels are popular for women.

Battle of the Bulge

The number of Americans who were extremely overweight, or obese, had been climbing steadily through the 1990s. By 2003, some states were claiming that more than one in every four people were considered obese. Many health care professionals suggested that more time spent driving, working jobs that were not physically demanding, and eating unhealthy food were major causes of weight gain. Across the country, people rose to the challenge of becoming healthy again. Health clubs gained popularity, and new companies selling exercise equipment and fitness advice emerged. People began eating more fresh, healthy food and buying less fast foods, such as burgers and fries. Eventually, fast food restaurants adapted to this trend as well, and started to offer healthier options as part of their menu.

Battle of the Bulge

Into the Future

In the 2000s, many trends took place online. Sites, such as Myspace and Facebook, allowed users to share information, music, and pictures with friends and family, regardless of their location. New technologies are always being developed to allow people to share information in interesting ways. Research online to see what the next big trend will be in communication.

2009   2010

Keep Rolling

skateboarding tricks on inline skates, and skaters used rails, boxes, stairs, and park benches as launching pads. Some inline skaters entered races that took place over many miles. There seemed no end to what Americans could do on inline skates. One thing they could do, unfortunately, was fall. Hospitals were filled with broken wrists, muscle pulls, and cuts and bruises from spills taken while inline skating. This led to a push for safe skating. Safety organizations encouraged skaters to wear helmets and wrist, knee, and elbow guards to prevent serious injuries. The message was generally well received, and Americans continued to enjoy inline skating into the 21st century.

1991

Cartoons Get Respect

In the 1990s, cartoons were no longer reserved for children on Saturday mornings. Cartoon feature films were reaching a new level of respect in Hollywood. In 1991, *Beauty and the Beast* astonished audiences with its incredible music and the realistic animation. The film was nominated for an Academy Award for Best Picture. It was the first time that a cartoon had reached that level of success. Other Disney films, including *The Little Mermaid*, *Aladdin*, and *The Lion King*, became hits

1990s

Keep Rolling

In the 1990s, inline skating became more and more popular. People were no longer just rolling on paths and sidewalks. They used inline skates to play roller hockey. Roller hockey leagues quickly spread across the country. Inline skate parks were also introduced. This gave people a chance to try

1991

Super Soaker water guns are a popular toy.

1992

Grunge fashion becomes a major trend.

Cartoons Get Respect

with both children and adults. Television also picked up on the animation trend, but its cartoons were made for adults. *The Simpsons* was an adult cartoon about a family of misfits. Bart, the young boy, was always in trouble and was quick with insults. Lisa was a scholar who did not fit in with her family. Homer, their father, was dim-witted and loved donuts. Marg, the mother, tried to keep her family in line, and Maggie, the baby, never said a word. *The Simpsons* was a huge hit, and its success brought more adult-focused cartoons, including *King of the Hill* and the controversial *South Park*. The language and content of many *South Park* episodes provided proof that cartoons were not just for kids.

1991

Tuned In

In the nineties, audiences had more television programs to choose from than ever before. By 1991, three-quarters of U.S. families had video cassette recorders (VCRs). The VCR was the fastest-selling piece of home-entertainment equipment in history. It offered a relatively inexpensive source of entertainment. More and more Americans were choosing to spend their Friday nights in front of their televisions. There were more than four billion movie rentals in the U.S. in 1991 alone. In some areas, movie watchers could order films from their homes. By 1992, cable television was exploding. Revenues for this service reached $22 billion. Viewers had countless channels with hundreds of comedies, dramas, and cultural programs running 24 hours a day.

Tuned In

1993
The first Beanie Babies hit the market.

1994
The Gap opens its discount clothing outlet Old Navy.

1995
The WB TV network premieres.

The Call of Coffee

1990s

The Call of Coffee

In the 1990s, Americans' heads were spinning with choices: mochaccino, cappuccino, decaf low-fat latté, and iced coffee. People were crazy for coffee. The beverage became more than just something to drink—it was a way of life. People gathered in coffee shops for business meetings or spent lazy Saturday afternoons with friends sipping fancy, and often expensive, drinks. Even those who did not have time to relax at coffee shops needed a shot of java to keep them going. Go-mugs and travel cups kept Americans in caffeine at all times. No matter where a person was, there was sure to be a coffee shop on the nearest corner. The coffee **phenomenon** spread to homes as well. Many Americans bought the coffee beans and special equipment that coffee shops used to make these drinks. A cappuccino machine was a must-have for many people in the 1990s. Americans spent many hours and dollars trying to brew the perfect cup of java.

1990s

Piercing What?

Traditionally, body piercing was a cultural practice. In the 1980s, it was mostly women who pierced their ears, sometimes having many piercings in one ear. By the 1990s, both males and females took part in the piercing craze. Piercings strayed from the traditional area, earlobes. They began showing up all over the body. The trend was to have metal in new areas such as eyebrows, noses, belly-buttons, tongues, and lips. Studs or rings adorned the faces of the nineties generation. Many parents thought their children's goal was to shock them, just as they had shocked their parents by wearing their hair long or their skirts short in the 1960s or 1970s. Many of the young people insisted that they were merely making fashion statements and showing their individuality with their pierced body parts. Their explanation was often not enough for parents, teachers, and employers. Many parents tried to prevent their children from getting pierced, while teachers and employers banned the rings. This did not stop the youth of the nineties. They took the rings out for their shift or during the school day and put them back in at the end of it. Body piercings were here to stay.

1996
Tamagotchi, a digital pet, makes it debut.

1997
Ty Beanie Babies are put in McDonald's Happy Meals.

1998
Furby, a toy robot, enters the market.

Piercing What?

Into the Future

Some trends have a longer life span than others. Television, piercings, and coffee are trends that have lasted a long time. Others, such as inline skating, have faded over time. Think about trends that you have experienced. Can you think of any that have disappeared? Which current trends do you think will last the longest? Why?

1999

Website www.blogger.com allows people to create their own web-logs, or "blogs."

2000

People prepare for Y2K.

Fitness Craze
Jane Fonda (right)

1981

Fitness Craze

In 1981, an Oscar-winning actor joined the fitness fad with the release of *Jane Fonda's Workout Book*. Fonda's book offered diet tips and exercise routines, and it gave general health information for women. Her book reached Americans who were aerobics crazy—mostly women who were eager to get into shape and be healthy. The book was a bestseller and was followed by cassette tapes of music to play while working out. There were also fitness studios and, later, a video to demonstrate the exercises. Americans handed over their money and cleared away the furniture in their family rooms so that they could "feel the burn" and shed the pounds. Many other people cashed in on the fitness craze. Sneaker manufacturers introduced running shoes made with extra support for exercising. Thousands of fitness clubs and gyms opened across the country to accommodate the growing number of men and women interested in bulking up or losing weight. Unlike many fads, the fitness craze continued for the rest of the century and into the next.

1981

Music Television, or MTV, begins broadcasting with the song "Video Killed the Radio Star."

1982

Coleco begins mass production of Cabbage Patch Kids.

1981

Rubik's Cube

Who would have imagined that a six-sided cube could cause so much fascination? Hungarian professor Erno Rubik had an idea that his Rubik's Cube would frustrate and delight puzzle lovers around the world. He invented the puzzle in 1975 as a way of teaching his students about **three-dimensional** objects. A few years later, he sold the puzzle worldwide. People first had to twist the rows of squares to scramble the colors. Then they had to figure out how to twist them back into position with only one color on each side. It seemed an impossible task at first. As the 1980s rolled on, people learned how to solve the puzzle. Then, they concentrated on solving it faster. Some Rubik's Cube wizards could solve the puzzle in less than a minute. By July 1981, 10 million cubes had been sold in the U.S. alone.

From Vinyl to Plastic

1982

From Vinyl to Plastic

In 1982, U.S. music lovers were introduced to a new, high-tech way of listening to albums. Cassette tapes and **vinyl** records were out. Compact disks were the way of the future. Americans were excited by the state-of-the-art CD. Phillips Corporation and Sony released their new lightweight disks, which promised the highest-quality recordings. The disks were very small, measuring 4.75 inches across rather than the 12 inches of albums. Music was recorded on each metallic pit on the disk. A CD player used a laser to read these pits and convert them into sound. Using a laser decreased wear on the disk, which made it last longer. CDs also held more information, or music, than a cassette or album could. They became popular and quickly took over the music market from vinyl records.

Rubik's Cube

1983

Care Bears become plush toys.

1984

The first issue of the *Teenage Mutant Ninja Turtles* comic book hits the stands.

1985

A hole in the ozone layer increases concern about the environment.

Break Dancing

The rise of rap music in the 1980s brought a new form of dancing to U.S. streets. Break dancing was introduced by inner-city African-American youth. Groups of people would gather at schoolyards or on street corners, turn up the hip-hop or rap music, and show off their moves. They often competed with each other, comparing their best tricks. Many did back flips and head spins. Others perfected jerky, robot-like maneuvers. Break dancing was so popular that movies were made about it. *Wild Style* (1982) paved the way for other break dancing movies, such as *Breakin'* (1984) and *Breakin' 2: Electric Boogaloo* (1984).

Break Dancing

Adopting Dolls

1983

Adopting Dolls

The adoption rate hit the roof in 1983. Young Americans gladly promised to give their Cabbage Patch Kids a good home. Each doll was a little different from the others and came with its own adoption certificate. Its owner became its adoptive parent. But getting these dolls home in the first place was not always easy— many people wanted them. There were riots in the stores as parents fought over the last dolls for their children. Some stores started wrapping the dolls in paper so that buyers would not fight over the ones they liked best. The Cabbage Patch craze went further to include clothing for the dolls and a younger generation of babies, including very small "preemie" babies.

1986
The Transformers: The Movie is released.

1987
Acid wash denim is popular with both men and women.

1988
Koosh balls are a common toy.

Strap on a Swatch

1983

Strap on a Swatch

Americans were telling time in style. Swiss company Asuag-SSIH hit it big with its line of durable watches, called Swatches. The company released Swatches to compete with cheap watches from Japan. Swatches were a hit. These ticking accessories became a must for Americans. The inexpensive plastic watches were available in many colors, patterns, and styles.

Into the Future

Recorded music has gone through many changes in format, from vinyl albums to 8 tracks, and finally, CDs. Many people today refer to CDs as the "last physical format." Much music listening in the future likely will happen through computers and music players, such as the iPod. Research technology trends to learn more about new music formats. What will be the wave of the future?

1989

The Nintendo Game Boy is developed.

1990

New Kids on the Block release many hit songs.

Downsizing

1970s

Hustlin'

Saturday nights were dance nights. Americans put on their platform shoes and bell-bottomed pants and swarmed the dance clubs. During the sixties, dancers had not needed partners. The seventies brought couples back to the dance floor. Some line dances could be danced alone, but most disco dances required two. Hot singers introduced a series of spins, turns, and steps to be done to their songs. Many disco enthusiasts took dancing seriously. Some rehearsed complicated dance moves during the week before trying them out on the dance floor. The bump, the hustle, and the robot were a few of the many dance crazes of the seventies.

Hustlin'

1970s

Downsizing

Since the Model T of the early 1900s, Americans have loved their automobiles. Many U.S. cars were big and comfortable—the bigger the car, the more successful the driver. With the 1970s energy crisis, big cars became a problem. Incredibly high oil prices, along with long line-ups and limits at the gas pumps, caused many Americans to look for more affordable ways to travel. People began buying smaller cars that would travel farther on a tank of gas. Many of these were foreign-built cars. They were easy to drive, economical, and more environmentally friendly than large cars.

1971

Tapestry by Carole King wins the 1971 Album of the Year Grammy.

1972

The first commercial video game is released by Magnavox.

1970s

Disco Skating

The disco trend did not stop when night clubs lost popularity. Disco filtered into the streets, where Americans welcomed the newest fad—roller disco. Roller skaters learned disco moves on skates and performed in parks and arenas. Disco music pumped through speakers or earphones, as disco skaters rolled. Many serious roller disco dancers in the late seventies dressed in stretchy, brightly colored satin pants and entered competitions at roller rinks and in parks. In the mid-seventies, roller skate wheels were being made from a hard plastic called polyurethane. These were quieter than metal or wooden wheels, and they allowed skaters to skate faster and more smoothly. Just as *Saturday Night Fever* had started the craze for disco, the movie *Roller Boogie* glorified roller disco.

1973	1974	1975
Three *Six Million Dollar Man* TV movies hit the airwaves.	*Happy Days* begins a 10-year run on TV.	Pets rocks are a brief fad.

Video Box

In 1975, Sony released its first video cassette recorders (VCRs). They were called Betamax. Later that year, Victor Company of Japan introduced the Video Home System (VHS). It quickly cornered the home entertainment market. No matter which machine Americans chose, the results were similar. People could record television programs and watch them later, often fast-forwarding through the commercials. New businesses sprouted up throughout the country offering pre-taped movies and programs for rent. This business boomed as Americans decided to watch movies in the comfort of their own homes. VCRs also gave rise to camcorders, which allowed Americans to video their families and friends and view the tapes on their home systems.

Fitness Fad Warms Up

Video Box

1978

Fitness Fad Warms Up

It started with editor James Fixx. He took up running to get in shape and then released his 1978 bestseller *The Complete Book of Running*. Soon, the entire nation was looking at getting into shape. Americans envied the discipline of **marathon** champion Bill Rogers. Rogers did more than inspire people to be fit. He also marketed a line of

1976
Punk rock music and fashion explode in Great Britain and New York.

1977
Star Wars is released in theaters.

1978
Garfield the cat makes his cartoon debut.

athletic clothing. Fitness clothing and equipment became a multi-billion dollar industry in the U.S., and Americans ran right alongside the trendsetters.

1978

Disco Fever

Americans borrowed many of their fads from the big screen. One of the biggest movies to influence society in the seventies was *Saturday Night Fever*. John Travolta starred as a young man in Brooklyn looking for his place on the dance floor. His style of dancing was disco. The release of the movie in 1978 created a disco craze across the country. Travolta's amazing dance moves and disco fashion inspired inner-city teens to dance, choosing the colored strobe lights and disco clubs over the streets. Dance clubs, such as Studio 54, became the "in" places to be. Hundreds

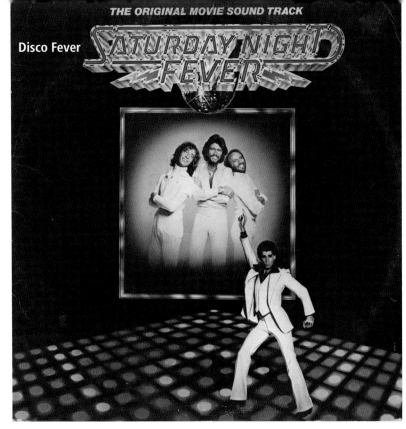

Disco Fever

THE ORIGINAL MOVIE SOUND TRACK

of people gathered at the club's doors every weekend, hoping that the doorman would choose them to join the party. By 1980, there were at least 10,000 discos in the U.S., and the industry earned more than $4 billion per year.

Into the Future

When the VCR was first released, some people thought the movie business would lose money. Instead, movie rentals brought increased earnings for the movie industry. Today, there are similar concerns about sharing movies online. In what ways can the movie industry use the Internet and movie sharing to make more money? What can be done to ensure that people do not share movies illegally?

1979

Disposable toothbrushes become available.

1980

Ted Turner launches CNN.

Trends
1960s

**Pop Art
Marilyn Monroe**

boxes delighted Americans. Warhol also mass-produced silk-screens of celebrities, including Marilyn Monroe, in many different colors. His exhibitions were instant sensations across the country. Warhol's experiences as a commercial illustrator opened the door for him to explore this unique form of art. Pop art not only had an impact on the art community, it also had an effect on commercial, graphic, and fashion design in the 1960s.

1960s

Let's Twist

In the 1960s, all a dancer needed was music. Partners were optional. A dance called the twist had been popular in the African-American community, but it took Chubby Checker to bring it to the rest of the country. This 20-year-old singer recorded "The Twist" and performed it on the television show American Bandstand. Then, Americans from all areas of the country took up twisting. It became a number-one hit with both teenagers and adults. Soon, spin-off songs and dances popped up, including the peppermint twist, the mashed potato, and the frug. Other popular dances were the hitchhiker, the monkey, and the jerk. All of these dances brought light-hearted fun and enthusiastic dancers to dance floors across the country.

1960s

Pop Art

Popular art, or pop art, began in response to abstract art in the 1940s and 1950s. Pop artists thought art should be drawn from real life. Their works were inspired by popular culture. While this style had existed in the fifties, it developed quickly in the sixties. One American artist built funny representations of fast food. Another reconstructed comic book frames using oils. Then Andy Warhol, who became a leading artist in the popular art revolution, took the genre a step further. He produced hundreds of works using silk-screening. His pictures of such everyday items as Campbell's Soup™ cans, Coca-Cola™ bottles, and Brillo™ soap pad

1961
Surf music makes its way to the airwaves, thanks to the Beach Boys.

1962
Millions of Americans sing along with Bob Dylan as he releases "Blowin' in the Wind."

1963
Troll dolls are a popular toy.

1964
Bell-bottom pants are seen in the film *The T.A.M.I. Show*.

1965
The lava lamp is first created.

Flower Power

The hippie movement became strong in many parts of the U.S., especially in the Haight-Ashbury district of San Francisco. Hippies saw themselves as separated from their parents' generation and did all they could to show it. They were not concerned with material goods and often shopped at second-hand stores or army surplus stores. To them, clothing was a necessity, not a sign of wealth. To further escape from and put down Western **capitalism**, they wore ethnic clothing. Many wore tribal patterns and styles borrowed from Eastern countries. Hippies followed Eastern philosophies and religions, some of which involved meditating. They made love beads and other ethnic jewelry popular. Through their actions, hippies tried to encourage peace and love, and they fought for social issues, including civil rights and the withdrawal of troops from Vietnam. Although the hippie movement represented only a small percentage of the U.S. population, its ideals and styles filtered into mainstream society.

Flower Power

1960s

Hats Off to Hair

Big really was beautiful in the 1960s, at least where hair was concerned. Women spent hours in front of their mirrors, with curlers, combs, and hair lacquer close at hand, trying to achieve the right height. First, they teased their hair with combs to give it the desired volume and sprayed it heavily to hold its shape. Then, they lifted the top layer of hair over the teased hair and sprayed it in place. This gave the hairstyle its height and hive shape. Many women washed their hair only once a

1966
Star Trek makes its
TV debut.

1967
The hippie culture
gains popularity.

1968
The Beatles star in
Yellow Submarine.

week. They kept the style in place by wearing carefully placed curlers at night and reteasing and spraying in the morning. The beehive style, which was a carry-over from the fifties, remained popular until the mid-sixties. Women who could not or did not want to wear a beehive often went for the bouffant look. Their hair was still full, but it was not pulled back into the final beehive shape. Women with this hairstyle still teased and sprayed to achieve the perfect look. First Lady Jacqueline Kennedy wore a toned-down bouffant hairdo and made this style a fashion must. With such large and elaborate hairstyles, most women left their hats at home. Those who wore hats chose ones that were big enough to fit over their huge hairdos, or they chose tiny pillbox hats that sat on top of the head.

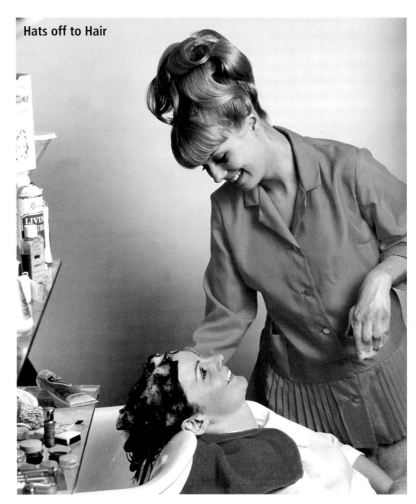

Hats off to Hair

Into the Future

The hippie movement was short-lived, but the ideals it promoted still exist today. Groups such as Greenpeace and the Sierra Club fight to protect the environment. The American Civil Liberties Union (ACLU) and Reporters Without Borders campaign for civil rights. Many groups are strong voices for peace. Dedicated people can even make careers out of trying to make the world a better place. Can you think of other groups that might have been inspired by the hippie movement?

1969

The Woodstock music festival plays to hundreds of thousands of people in New York state.

1970

"Do the Funky Chicken" becomes a hit song and dance craze.

1950s

Feel the Beat

The "Beat Generation" came out of the 1950s. Many of these people had fought in the Korean War and did not believe in the American Dream anymore. "Beat," to them, meant beaten. The beatniks originated in San Francisco and Los Angeles. They were easy to spot. The men wore beards and short hair. They usually sported khaki pants, sweaters, and sandals. Women wore black leotards or long dresses. Beatniks loved jazz and wrote poetry, and they often read it in coffee houses with drums or other instruments accompanying them. Jack Kerouac was a leader who tried to explain that the beatniks loved everything and were not the radicals the "squares" thought they were. He wrote one of the most famous beat books, *On the Road*, which sold 500,000 copies. The book is about friendship and wanderings, and Kerouac wrote it in just three weeks.

Feel the Beat
Jack Kerouac

1950s

Dance Floor Dynamos

The fifties were a great time for dancing. There were many different dances that often went with the hit songs of the time. The hand jive, danced to a song of the same name, was a series of claps, hand movements, foot steps, and kicks. Like most dances of the decade, the hand jive was often done with a partner. Jiving came out of

1951
The first color television shows are broadcast.

1952
Full skirts give way to slim-fitting pencil skirts.

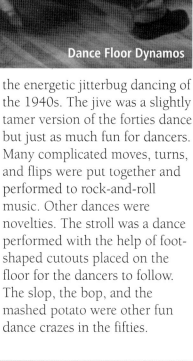

Dance Floor Dynamos

College Cramming

In the 1950s, college cramming had nothing to do with studying. Students would try to stuff as many bodies as possible into the tightest places. Across the country, college campuses were packed with students trying to set records by fitting as many people or objects as possible in the smallest space possible. At one California college, 22 students managed to stuff themselves into a phone booth. At another, 40 students filled a Volkswagon Beetle. At Caltech, two students filled their room with newspaper. This crazy spring tradition swept the U.S. in the late fifties and was abandoned in the sixties.

College Cramming

the energetic jitterbug dancing of the 1940s. The jive was a slightly tamer version of the forties dance but just as much fun for dancers. Many complicated moves, turns, and flips were put together and performed to rock-and-roll music. Other dances were novelties. The stroll was a dance performed with the help of foot-shaped cutouts placed on the floor for the dancers to follow. The slop, the bop, and the mashed potato were other fun dance crazes in the fifties.

1953
The first TV dinners are sold.

1954
The first transistor radios are available on the market.

1955
Pez aims their product at children.

3-D Movies

1952

3-D Movies

In 1952, the movie industry found that its audiences had been reduced by about half because people were watching the new invention, television. Movie producers needed a way to draw people back to the theaters. It found one. The National Vision Corporation thought up a movie idea called three-dimensional, or 3-D. By projecting overlapping images onto the screen, the company made the pictures look as if the action were happening right there. This only worked if the audience wore Polaroid glasses that brought the images back together again. The first full-length 3-D movie was shown in Los Angeles on November 26, 1952. *Bwana Devil* made a record $95,000 in its first week. Audiences loved the effect of characters jumping out at them. The fad exploded in the U.S. and then faded quickly. The novelty of 3-D movies could no longer support the low-budget plots, so studios stopped producing them.

1958

Hula Hoop

In 1958, a California toymaker caught wind of an Australian game used in gym classes—students exercised by spinning bamboo hoops around their waists. The toymaker decided to try it in the U.S. From the moment they began selling, the $1.98 hula hoops were a phenomenon. Within six months, 30 million hoops were sold. The fad started in California and quickly worked its way across the country. A 10-year-old boy in New Jersey set a record with 3,000 consecutive spins. The country was hoop-crazy, and it was not only children

Hula Hoop

1956

The first go kart is built.

1957

Sea Monkeys are first sold under the name Instant Life.

1958

The first Grammy Awards take place.

getting in on the fun. Adults spun the hoops, too. People could not get enough of hula hoops, for a while, at least. Like any fad, this one soon lost its popularity. The end of the summer brought the end of the craze. Children still played with hula hoops, but they were no longer a must-have.

1959

America's New Doll

In March 1959, children had a new playmate. Mattel Toys launched their new toy doll named Barbie. The 11.5-inch doll sold for $3.00. As sales of the doll rocketed, different Barbies were released, all with different clothing and accessories. Barbie was given a boyfriend, Ken, in 1961 and then many friends in the years to come. Barbie has become the most successful doll in history, selling hundreds of millions of dolls around the world.

America's New Doll

Into the Future

Some trends, such as Barbie dolls and hula hoops, have been popular for decades. Others, such as the jive, fizzle after a short time. Think about the trends you see around you today. Which do you think will have staying power? Why?

1959

Pantyhose are created.

1960

Tower Records, the first music megastore, opens in Sacramento, California.

1940s

Dancing the Night Away

Dancing the Night Away

Despite the worry and fear brought by the war, Americans could lift their spirits at the dance halls. The jitterbug helped chase away the fears of American boys overseas, even if only for an evening. This swing dance had been popular in the 1930s but became a worldwide sensation in the forties. American servicemen spread the dance to the countries where they were stationed. It was a hit at home, too. Partners often held both hands and did different dance steps and acrobatic swings. They usually made up their own steps. This high-energy dance was best performed to the music of swing bands or their records. Even the musicians who played in dance halls every week could not say exactly which moves made up the jitterbug. Americans did not mind—they just wanted to spend their weekends spinning, flipping, and tapping their toes to hot forties swing music.

Slumber Parties

In the 1940s, Friday nights were meant for friends. Nothing brought a group of

1941

Silk stockings are banned, so women apply colored foundation to shade their legs.

1942

Food rationing begins across the United States.

girls closer than weekly sleep-overs. The teens dressed in their fathers' oversized pajamas or nightshirts and spent the evening talking. They discussed what they had read in teen magazines and took turns reading from their favorite articles. The girls did not neglect their beauty treatments during these parties. They still applied nightly mud masks to clear their skin and did their hair up in curlers or pins. The teens burned extra energy by having pillow fights before trying to sleep. These slumber parties were held across the country.

1943
Disc jockeys begin spinning records for U.S. troops overseas.

1944
Seventeen magazine is published for the first time.

1945
Earl Tupper creates Tupperware plastic containers. **31**

Risky Business
Louis Réard

1946

Risky Business

In 1946, many women looked to Louis Réard's invention to shake up their summer. Réard had created the two-piece bathing suit. Many people thought these bathing suits immodest because they did not cover nearly as much of women's bodies as previous suits. Others found the new suits liberating, not to mention attention-getting! Mediterranean beaches were the first to be invaded by two-piece suits, and the trend soon hit American shores. The suits were called bikinis. Their name came from the Bikini Atoll, which is an island in the South Pacific. Bikini is where Americans tested nuclear weapons. People said bikini suits caused as much commotion as the explosions.

1946

Jukebox Junkies

Teenagers in the forties had money to spend. So advertisers and manufacturers began to focus on this important market. Many teens held jobs to support the war effort, and on Saturday nights they liked to spend their money in dance halls. This provided a boost to the music industry. By 1946, record companies were selling ten times more songs than they had sold ten years earlier. The major studios, such as RCA and Decca, sold 100 million records each year. With the new long-playing 45-rpm and 33-rpm records, jukeboxes became a major industry. They brought in about five billion nickels each year. Teens could listen to jukebox music at their favorite soda shop before heading to the dance hall, where they practiced their lindy and jitterbug dance moves.

1948

Music Made Easy

For Americans who loved to listen to music at home, 1948 was an important year.

1946
The microwave oven is invented by Percy Spencer.

1947
The first unidentified flying object (UFO) sighting is publicized in the U.S. media.

1948
Leo Fender invents the electric guitar.

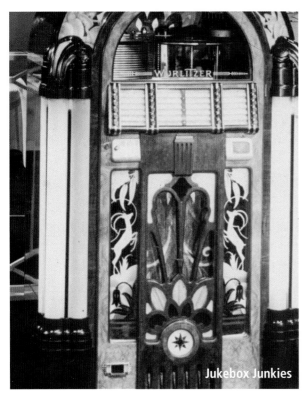

Jukebox Junkies

Music Made Easy

Columbia Records released a new 12-inch vinyl record. These new records had smaller grooves and played at 33 1/3 revolutions per minute (rpm) instead of the previous 78 revolutions. They were called long-playing records, or LPs, because they offered 25 minutes of music per side instead of the three to five minutes of previous records. This meant they could contain several songs instead of just one or two. LPs boasted improved sound quality, so music lovers could feel almost as if they had a live band playing in their own home. LPs dominated music for more than 30 years, until the arrival of compact discs.

Into the Future

Certain trends change form over time. Dancing, for example, has always been part of society, from the earliest recorded history. Dances themselves, however, have changed throughout history. Think about how you or your friends dance. How is it the same or different from dances done in past decades? What do you think the next big dance craze will be? Will it change the way you move to music?

1949

The Volkswagen Beetle becomes the first foreign car, and the first compact car, sold in the United States.

1950

Kraft begins selling sliced processed cheese.

1930s

Picture Pages Premiere

In the thirties, Americans were introduced to a new form of entertainment—comic books. Within the pages of these books, there were many heroes to read about. Some were superheroes like Flash Gordon. Flash Gordon had been an ivy-league polo player before he and beauty Dale Arden were kidnapped on the rocket of crazy Dr. Hans Zarkov. *Flash Gordon* was so popular that the comic book was made into a movie, starring Buster Crabbe. Other heroes battled evil on Earth. Dick Tracy was a tough detective who fought gangsters. Americans welcomed this trigger-happy crime fighter as they watched real-life gangsters get away with their crimes. The *Dick Tracy* comic strip marked the first time someone had been shot in the funny pages. The take-no-bull detective was soon on the radio fighting gangsters and selling boxes and boxes of Quaker Oats cereal for the show's sponsor.

1932

Drive-In Movies

Richard Hollingshead knew he had a great idea when he hung a sheet in his backyard. He put a radio behind this screen and added cars to the equation. Hollingshead applied for a

Picture Pages Premiere

1931
"The Star Spangled Banner" becomes the U.S. national anthem.

1932
Gospel music makes its debut.

patent for a drive-in movie theater in 1932. He was awarded a patent and the first drive-in theater opened in Camden, New Jersey, on June 6, 1933. Similar theaters were built in many states, including Pennsylvania, Texas, California, Massachusetts, Rhode Island, Florida, and Michigan. Throughout the thirties, Americans paid to watch movies in the comfort of their own cars. Friends packed into cars and headed to drive-in movie theaters on Friday and Saturday nights. The drive-in movie craze continued to attract audiences in large numbers for several decades.

Drive-In Movies

1933
The first drive-in movie theater opens in New Jersey.

1934
Multiple-selection jukeboxes are introduced by Wurlitzer.

1935
Parking meters make their first appearance on U.S. streets.

35

1930s

Trendsetting Inventor

Leo Seltzer knew what people wanted. He made dance marathons an exciting, yet sometimes painful, activity in the thirties. In those hard times, dancers saw marathons as a way to escape. Prize money was often between $1,000 and $5,000—a huge amount of money for the time. The catch was that dancers had to keep moving. These contests could last for weeks, with couples dragging rather than dancing their way around the hall. The competition ended when there was only one couple left standing among the heaps of exhausted contestants. The winners split the prize money and were hailed as local heroes. Those who did not compete filled the room to watch the contest, cheering on their favorite couples. Dance marathons attracted huge crowds and were a popular event during the decade. Seltzer next thought of combining dance derbies with the roller-skating fad. He came up with the roller derby. People who competed in the roller derby skated around a sloped track for 60,000 laps—the equivalent distance of New York to Los Angeles. During the first week of the roller derby in 1935, about 20,000 people paid to watch the contest. Men and women competed around the country. Soon, Seltzer decided to change the derby to make it more entertaining. He legalized elbowing, pushing, hair-pulling, and other violent means to get ahead. He also added other forms of entertainment and staged fights to liven up the show. Crowds could not get enough of the performances. Roller derby has faded and been revived many times since the 1930s. Leo Seltzer's son, Jerry, brought back the sport in the 1990s with "Roller Jam."

1936
Shopping carts are made available to shoppers in the United States.

1937
Walt Disney releases *Snow White and the Seven Dwarfs*.

1938
The process for making photocopies is invented.

Feeling the Music

In 1937, Lee David and John Redmond wrote "The Big Apple"—a sensation that would quickly become a craze. This swing song had moves that dancers performed, often while dancing in a circle. The dancers followed the lead caller, doing the "Suzi-Q," "truckin'," and old square dancing moves, including the London Bridge. When the caller told the enthusiastic dancers to "Praise Allah," they leaned back and threw their hands in the air. Thirties dancers all over the country trucked to the left, stomped, and swung to "The Big Apple." Swingers did not need to be at dance halls to be "in the groove." Many could have fun "truckin'" anywhere they went. Truckin' was a swing phenomenon enjoyed by students and swingers alike. It was a finger-waving, hip-swaying walk that set the "hepcats" apart from the uninformed "longhairs."

Feeling the Music

Into the Future

From *Snow White and the Seven Dwarfs* to *The Simpsons*, animated characters have come a long way since their debut. Today, there are comics for every age and interest. Telling stories with pictures is an ancient art form. How have people used drawings to tell stories throughout history? How is art used today to express thoughts and ideas?

1939

Air conditioning becomes an option in cars.

1940

One of the first game shows, a radio quiz on the CBS network, hits the airwaves.

1923

A Game From Abroad

It started in California and then took over the country. Mah-jongg was everywhere. This traditional Mandarin game was brought from China after World War I by an American missionary. Americans were intrigued by Asia, so Asian styles or culture were a definite hit. The missionary changed the game slightly and copyrighted it. At the height of the mah-jongg craze in 1923, about 10 million women met regularly at mah-jongg parties and 1.6 million sets were sold.

A Game From Abroad

The Good Times Roll

1920s

The Good Times Roll

After World War I, Americans were ready to let loose and have fun. They had more time on their hands. The workweek was reduced from 60 to 48 hours. Wages were increased, giving Americans more money to spend. Products and fads reached the population quickly, thanks to mass marketing with ads on the radio and in newspapers. Those who could not afford a product used the new "installment plan." They could buy anything on credit—from a toaster to a new car.

1921
The first shopping mall opens near Kansas City.

1922
Time Magazine begins publication.

1923
The song "The Charleston" is released, creating a dance craze.

38

The Latest Steps

The Charleston started out as an African-American folk dance. In 1923, it was changed for Broadway's production of *Runnin' Wild*. The lively dance became an instant sensation. Across the country, dancers were slapping their knees, swaying their hips, and swinging their legs to the Charleston. It could be danced alone or with a partner, and it became a social necessity—those who could not do the Charleston were left sitting on the sidelines at social functions. The older generation did not approve. Many thought the way women showed their legs and kicked their feet was indecent. The Charleston was banned in some towns. These bans only made the dance more appealing. Variations of the dance were quickly created, including the Varsity Drag, the Black Bottom, and the Shimmy. Like many fads, the Charleston craze soon died.

The Latest Steps

1924
Two movie studios merge to form one of the largest studios to date, MGM.

1925
Art deco becomes popular around the world.

39

Sweet Tooth Satisfied

1923

Sweet Tooth Satisfied

During the twenties, Americans' need for sweets was easily met. Cans and boxes replaced jars, making it less expensive to package and purchase goods. In 1923, Jell-O hit supermarket shelves. This jiggly treat had been around for more than 20 years, but only now was it given the brand name. Ice cream also experienced a revolution. As well as the usual ice cream cones, there were now specialty bars and cones. The Good Humor Bar, the Popsicle, and the Eskimo Pie all made their appearance in the 1920s. The Eskimo Pie sold one million bars a day in its second year on sale. There were also new candies. Americans could pick up Mounds, Milky Way, and Reese's Peanut Butter Cups by 1923. To wash these treats down, companies created bubbly, sweet sodas. The 1920 clear soda called Howdy was renamed 7-Up a few years later. For the do-it-yourself Americans, a new drink that was mixed at home hit the market in 1927. By adding sugar and water to the flavored powder, Americans made their own Kool-Aid. This became a popular way to beat the summer heat.

1926
The first "talkie" films are introduced.

1927
The first jukeboxes are sold.

1928
Walter Deimer, an accountant from Philadelphia, invents bubblegum.

Six-Letter Word for Fun

Millions of Americans tested their vocabularies with the newest fad—crossword puzzles. The rise in popularity of crossword puzzles led to the rise of one of the biggest publishing houses in the world—Simon & Schuster. The company was formed in 1924 to publish the first collection of crossword puzzles ever printed as a book. These portable puzzles were a great way for people to pass the time while waiting for a bus or sitting on a train on their way to or from work. The books came with a sharpened pencil so that the puzzles could be solved immediately. The puzzle books sold nearly a million copies in one year. While there had been puzzles in newspapers and magazines for years, the public was thrilled to have them in book form. They became one of the biggest trends of the time. A six-letter word for fun in the twenties was "puzzle."

Into the Future

Many games in the 2000s require batteries or electricity, but this technology did not always exist. Card games, word puzzles, and games with specialized pieces, such as chess or Mahjongg, have been enjoyed for decades. What other games did people play without the use of technology? Are any of these games still played today?

1929

The original 7-Up drink is first marketed.

1930

Betty Boop makes her debut.

Trends
1910s

1910

Fun and Games

Before the 1910s, most stores carried toys only at Christmas time. By the end of the decade, toys and games were on store shelves year-round. Transportation toys were popular. The friction auto racer was a toy car that could climb. It ran backward and forward. Toy airplanes were on many boys' wish lists as well. The airplanes flew in circles as their propellers whirled. A milk wagon with turning rubber wheels was another hit with children. Building kits, porcelain dolls, board games, and magic sets also delighted U.S. children. One of the most popular toys of the

1910s was the Humpty Dumpty Circus. The small figures of lion tamers, clowns, trick riders, elephants, and other circus animals could all be arranged in different ways with their movable heads and limbs.

1914

Care to Dance?

Americans celebrated the good economic times in the early 1910s by crowding onto the dance floor. In 1914, the fox trot took over every dance hall in the country. It combined the energy of ragtime music with the elegance of high society. The fox trot became a symbol of modern Americans. The dance got its name from a vaudeville entertainer named Harry Fox, who added a trotting step to his routine. When the dance hit ballrooms, it involved two walking steps, a side step, and a quarter turn. The fox trot had many variations. Well-known dancer Irene Castle and her husband, Vernon, created a faster and more subtle version of the dance. Legend has it that Castle's dress was too tight at the bottom to perform the dance as it was usually done, so the pair

Care to Dance

accidentally changed it. They used the "Castle walk" in Broadway musicals, cabarets, and dance demonstrations.

1914

In the Driver's Seat

Horses and buggies were quickly becoming a thing of the past. Automobiles were the way of the future. They were no longer just luxury items reserved for wealthy people. The Model T, produced by automobile maker Henry Ford, was a fairly low-cost car. In 1914, Ford produced 240,700 Model Ts—nearly as

Fun and Games

1912
The world's first blues record is pressed.

1914
Jerome Kern blends music, ballet, and drama to create musical theater.

In the Driver's Seat

many cars as all the other automobile manufacturers combined. These cars, nicknamed Tin Lizzies, were simple machines, with strong steel frames. They were great on muddy streets and could travel at around 40 miles per hour on flat roads. If there were any problems with the car or its parts, drivers could easily fix them using the most basic tools—a screwdriver, hammer, wrench, and wire. Ford Motor Company even provided replacement parts. It sold mufflers for a quarter and a whole bumper for $2.50. As Ford streamlined his factories, the price of a Model T dropped. By 1916, Americans could drive one home for only $360. By the end of the 1910s, four million Tin Lizzies were puttering around U.S. streets.

1916

Movie Madness

In the 1910s, a night out at the theater no longer meant the opera or a play. Motion pictures were all the rage. Beautiful movie theaters were built. Patrons paid a few cents at the door and were welcomed with large, comfortable seats, elaborate decorations, and uniformed ushers. There was even a 25 piece orchestra to entertain them before the film began. Americans packed movie houses to watch the popular comedies and melodramas. For the first time, actors were recognized by name rather than by their studio. The "Biograph Girl" and "Vitagraph Girl" were finally revealed and became major box-office draws. Their huge salaries were met with huge profits. In 1916, about 25 million people each day paid between a dime and a quarter each to watch a movie. This brought more than $735 million to studios. Producers used this money to create more sophisticated, high-budget silent movies. In 1910, the common, one-reel movie cost studios about $500 to produce in only a few days. By the end of the decade, producers were releasing two-hour feature films that cost up to $20,000 to make. The motion-picture business was no longer a struggling industry run by a few competing studios. It was the fifth-largest industry in the country.

Movie Madness

Pedal Power

1900

Point and Click

In 1900, the Eastman Kodak Company announced, "You press the button, we do the rest." The new box camera called the Brownie made photography available to a wider group of people. It was small and easy to use, which the company hoped would appeal to young Americans. With the simplicity and fun of the Brownie, even children could now take pictures. At the cost of $1, the Brownie gave the user good-quality photographs without having to focus or time the exposure. To sweeten the appeal, Kodak said it would develop the film so amateurs would not have to battle with the mysteries of darkrooms. This marked the emergence of the shapshot.

Point and Click

AN EFFICIENT
5/-
FILM CAMERA.

THE BROWNIE.

Not a Toy. Takes splendid Photographs, 2¼ by 2¼ inches. Complete with Handbook of Instructions. Price only **5/-**

Of all Photographic Dealers, or from—

KODAK, Limited,

43, Clerkenwell Road, E.C.;
60, Cheapside, E.C.;
115, Oxford Street, W.;
and 171-3, Regent Street, W.

1900s

Pedal Power

The invention of the modern bicycle caused a buzz around the world. It was an inexpensive form of transportation and a great way to get exercise. Doctors relied on bicycles to do their house calls. Boys working for telegraph companies raced through the streets on their bicycles to deliver messages. The bicycle also changed the way people lived. Automobiles were just a fantasy for most Americans, but bicycles made it easy for them to get around. Employees could now live farther from the hustle and bustle of the inner city. They traveled to work and back on their bicycles. Cycling through the country became a weekend vacation idea. Families enjoyed the freedom offered by these new vehicles.

1909

Cute Little Kewpies

Rose O'Neill was well known for her drawings of adorable chubby angels with pointed heads. This talent led to an international sensation. In 1909, she made her art three-dimensional with the Kewpie doll. It was one of the

---

1901	**1903**	**1905**
King C. Gillette invents the disposable razor.	The Wright Brothers complete successful test flights of the airplane.	The windshield wiper is patented.

Cute Little Kewpies

She was one of the most popular and in-demand magazine illustrators—not to mention the highest paid female illustrator—in the country.

How Sweet It Is

Milton Snavely Hershey began his career in chocolate in 1893. He bought a German chocolate-making machine and started producing chocolate-covered caramels. The next year, he created the Hershey Chocolate Company to make cocoa, baker's chocolate, and sweet chocolate. Later, he sold the caramel business for $1 million and focused solely on chocolate. In 1903, Hershey began the two-year construction of a new chocolate factory in his hometown of Derry Church, Pennsylvania. He had promised people chocolate, he said, and chocolate they would get!

first character dolls—those based on a real person or personality—in the U.S. Originally, the dolls were made of **celluloid**. Little girls around the globe loved their Kewpie dolls. The demand was incredible, and the public insisted on more Kewpie dolls. These darlings were soon made from many materials, from **bisque** to chocolate. At one time, there were 36 factories in Germany devoted to producing bisque Kewpie dolls. To meet society's need for all things Kewpie, other products were soon released. Kewpie greeting cards, tableware, and jewelry flew off the shelves. This fad remained strong for nearly 20 years. It also served Rose O'Neill well. She earned more than $2 million in royalties from companies creating Kewpie

products. Her popularity spread from dolls to other areas. O'Neill also wrote four novels, several short stories, a collection of poetry, and many children's books. She illustrated all these works with her own drawings.

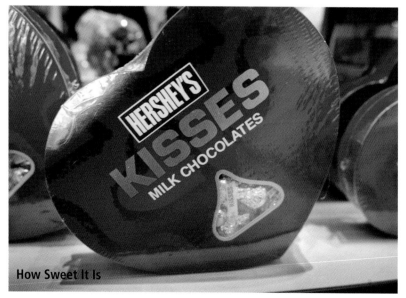

How Sweet It Is

Into the future

Trends have a unique ability to catch people's attention. Often, trends relate to the culture that produces them. In rare cases, very large and important trends can affect culture, as well. One of the most important features of a trend is how people think about and relate to it everyday.

There are two important ways in which people become aware of trends. First, trends can spread through word of mouth. People see someone else doing, wearing, listening to, or watching something new, and they decide to do the same thing. This is how The Beatles and the hippie movement first gained popularity. Trends such as these have a natural appeal that attracts people to them. Another way trends can become common is when people make an effort to tell others about a product. This is usually done through advertising, such as television commercials or ads in newspapers. Trends such as the Barbie doll and hula-hoop were made popular using this method.

Think about the trends around you. What is popular now that was not a short time ago? Are there any products, bands, television shows, or clothing styles that you think might grow in popularity over time? Many people make their living examining trends in the economy, politics, or on TV. Thinking about and predicting trends is an important skill in many careers, from journalism to science.

Spread Your Message

Many trends begin as good ideas that their creators hope will become popular. Is there something new that you enjoy doing, watching, or wearing? Think of ways you could help make this item a trend. How would you spread the word to others? Trends need to be seen by many people to become popular. A commercial might be a good way to send your message to many people at once. With friends, use a video camera or computer to record a commercial for this product. Next, try writing a newspaper article. Remember to include where the product came from, who created it, what it is, and when it was first introduced to the public. Post your article on the Internet, or give copies to friends. What other ways can you think of to share your message with others? The method you use can be as unique as the message itself.

FURTHER
Research

Many books and websites provide information on trends. To learn more about this topic, borrow books from the library, or surf the Internet.

Books

Most libraries have computers that connect to a database for researching information. If you input a key word, you will be provided with a list of books in the library that contain information on that topic. Non-fiction books are arranged numerically, using their call number. Fiction books are organized alphabetically by the author's last name.

Websites

To learn more about trends throughout history, visit **www.crazyfads.com**.

For information about fun fads from the 20th century, surf to **www.badfads.com**.

Glossary

bisque: unglazed china

capitalism: an economic system in which private owners control trade and industry for profit

celluloid: a type of plastic

global positioning systems: devices that use time and distance to calculate location by sending signals to and from satellites

marathon: a type of race or contest that takes lace over a long distance or extended period of time

phenomenon: something remarkable

three-dimensional: showing length, width, and depth

uninhabited: a place where humans do not live

vinyl: a type of plastic

Index